P9-EDK-477

EMILY BLISS

MARY AMES

From A NEW ENGLAND WOMAN'S DIARY *in* DIXIE
in 1865

By
MARY AMES

NEGRO UNIVERSITIES PRESS
NEW YORK

Originally published in 1906

Reprinted 1969 by
Negro Universities Press
A DIVISION OF GREENWOOD PUBLISHING CORP.
NEW YORK

SBN 8371-1386-5

PRINTED IN UNITED STATES OF AMERICA

INTRODUCTION

Some of Miss Ames's friends, who have enjoyed listening to the stories of her southern school life, have frequently begged her to print them.

This opportunity of helping to educate a pupil in that wonderful school, which is so great a contrast to the scene of her early efforts, has decided her to allow the diary to be prepared for publication.

In making this gift to Hampton, she emphasizes her first gift to the negro of eighteen months' service, and perpetuates the memory of the sister who was her closest friend and dearest companion, and whom Springfield will long remember as strong and brave and helpful; but especially will she be remembered for "her wit that woke their laughter and left a kindly glow." Even the boy who left the daily paper at her door felt her kindness and "caught the secret of her character."

On the day of her funeral, in June, 1903, he left three roses at the house, with the following words:

> " ' She doeth little kindnesses
> Which most leave undone or despise;
> For naught that sets one heart at ease
> And giveth happiness and peace
> Is low esteemed in her eyes.'
>
> From the morning newsboy, for whom she placed out such splendid apples."

JUNE, 1906.   E. L. C.

FROM A NEW ENGLAND WOMAN'S DIARY IN DIXIE IN 1865

MISS WARE, of Cambridge, came to Springfield to visit Mrs. Farrar. The story of her experiences with the colored people in the South was so interesting that my friend Emily Bliss and I became enthusiastic to follow her example.

We went to Boston, saw the chief of the Freedmen's Bureau, were examined, and enrolled as teachers.

We were ordered to leave at once for Hilton Head, and report to Mr. Dodge, the agent there. Our families ridiculed our going and tried to stop us, prophesying our return in less than a month. We made our preparations, which were not elaborate, — a chair, a plate, knife, fork and spoon; cup and saucer, blanket, sheets and pillow-cases, and sacking for a bed of hay or straw to be found wherever we should be situated, and we added some crackers, tea, and a teapot.

We sailed from New York on the steamer *Fulton*, May 1, 1865, and after a pleasant sail reached Hilton Head on the morning of the fourth day.

We landed after breakfast, and walked to the place where we took the oath of allegiance to the United States. We called upon Mr. Dodge, and found with him five or six teachers. We were not cordially received, and evidently were not wanted, and were advised to proceed to Charleston and report to Mr. Redpath, who was in charge of the Freedmen's Bureau there.

We met a Mr. Blake from New Haven, a pleasant young man, who offered to escort us to Charleston. He is employed by the Boston society to look after forlorn females who come as teachers.

At eight in the evening, we left Hilton Head on a small steamer loaded with soldiers on their way to Charleston, to be discharged from service. There was no place for us. We had to sit the long night through, on a bench with no back, surrounded by soldiers smoking, playing cards, and telling stories — the longest night I ever knew.

Arriving at Charleston early in the morning, we were taken to Mr. Redpath's office. He being absent, Mr. Pillsbury, of Massachusetts, came to meet us. He gave us a most cordial greeting.

Emily, weary, discouraged, and homesick, threw herself sobbing into his arms, saying, "Oh! sir, have you a wife?"

At once, he took in the situation, called an ambulance, and put us in charge of a sergeant with a note to his wife.

Mrs. Pillsbury, a lovely, motherly woman, took us in and made us comfortable. They were living in one of the most elegant mansions in Charleston; the furniture, pictures, and ornaments were all as their owner had left them. The garden was a delight; I never saw finer roses.

Mr. Redpath came to see us in the evening, wished us to remain in the city and teach in the public schools, and was quite disturbed and disappointed that we objected. We felt that we were not fitted for regular teaching. We were then offered a position on one of the islands where several thousand negroes were sent after Sherman's march. That suited us, and we were ordered to leave in two days.

Meanwhile, we visited different schools, and saw how *un*fitted we were for teachers.

MAY 10, 1865.

At one o'clock we left Charleston on the propeller *Hudson*, for Edisto Island. Sailing along the shore and up Edisto River, we reached the landing-place just at sunset.

It seemed like fairy land — everything so fresh and green — the air so soft.

We brought on the boat a hundred and fifty negroes, who, as soon as they landed, built fires to cook their supper;

the live-oaks in the background, with their hanging moss, had a very picturesque effect.

We spent the night on the boat, the captain giving us his stateroom. We had a visit from a Mrs. Webb and one of the officers of the 32d Regulars, colored infantry, two companies of which are stationed here to protect the island from guerrillas. We were asked to breakfast at headquarters, about half a mile from the landing.

MAY 11.

At seven we started for camp, which was on the plantation formerly owned by William Seabrook. They gave us a good breakfast; then the Colonel placed

7

at our disposal a large army wagon, drawn by four horses, to take us with our trunks and boxes to find a place to live. The drive was delightful, the road shaded and cool, winding under immense live-oak trees covered with moss; the wild grape was in bloom, and the air filled with its perfume. We passed several houses crowded with negroes, and could not make up our minds to stop at any. We drove on some three or four miles further and, as it began to be very warm and uncomfortable, we decided to stop at the very next house, negroes or no negroes. Soon we reached what must have once been a pretty avenue, now rather forlorn. Driving in, we found negro cabins on either side, and a large house at the end.

The inhabitants of the cabins came flocking out to welcome us with howdys, and offers of service to the missis. The former owner of the plantation was Dr. Whaley, the possessor of a hundred slaves, many of whom were now returned and living in the cabins. He deserted the place four years before, and the house had a desolate appearance — the windows gone, and shutters hanging by one hinge. Our trunks, box, and chairs were placed on the piazza and the army wagon was driven away. We looked at each other; our hearts were full, and if we could have seen any

9

honorable way to escape and go home we certainly should have gone.

However, we choked down our feelings, and the front door being opened by a black man and a woman, with half a dozen children hanging to her skirts, we entered our home to be. The rooms were large and airy (minus windows), but filled with sticks, plaster from the ceilings, and dirt of all kinds. We selected two rooms and asked if they could be cleared and cleaned. Uncle Jack and Aunt Phœbe, who lived in one of the cabins, came to our assistance, and having no brooms, mops, or any conveniences for cleaning, managed with the gray moss to wipe off the upper dust from the floors; then dashing on cold water, and with their feet shuffling the moss, contrived to wash the floors decently clean.

Meanwhile, the woman, Sarah, made the tea, which, with some crackers, we took out of our trunk; — and this, the first meal in our new home, we ate on the piazza. It was fortunate that we had chairs. The bedsteads were accidentally left behind in New York, but were to be sent on the next steamer. We spread our bed-sacks on the floor after it was dry, for we soon learned there was neither hay nor straw to be had to fill them, covered them with our waterproofs, and, as we had blankets and pillows, our beds were soon ready.

About sundown Mr. Blake appeared, and with him two young women teachers, also members of the Freedmen's Bureau. They brought a few blackberries, picked by the roadside, which were a welcome addition to our crackers and tea. On our way up-stairs to bed, we were met by an angry old woman, who said we had taken possession of her quarters, and must pay her for them. We were frightened, and explained that we were sent by the United States Government, and must be respected accordingly. She went away, but soon began to throw stones and pieces of crockery into our open windows. We were alarmed, for we did not know how many were leagued with her. It began to rain and a heavy thunder shower soon dispersed our assailants. But sleep was impossible. Having no doors to close, we did not know what might happen in a strange land among strange people. I got out the hammer we had brought in our box and kept it in my hand all night, ready to beat out the brains of any one attacking us.

MAY 12.

The first thing we did this morning was to get our flag hung out in front of the house. It is quite large and floated out finely. The negroes appeared glad to see it. We unpacked the big box, turning it on

13

its side to serve for a table and wash-stand.

Jim and Sarah, with six children, are living in the back part of this house. We are glad to have them for protection, and find them useful.

Sarah is a fine-looking woman, quiet and sensible. She has always been a house-servant, was born and reared in Richmond, was sold with three children to Dr. Leavitt of Charleston, leaving the father of her children in Richmond. Since that, she has had six children, having had five husbands, or men with whom she was obliged to live, as she was sold from one master to another. Jim was the last one. At the beginning of the war, Sarah and

14

her children were sent with her mistress to Sumterville.

When Sherman and his army came along, Sarah was told by her mistress that if she followed the army she must take all her children, not thinking she would go.

When the mistress found that Jim and Sarah were actually going, she asked one of the Union officers to make Sarah stay behind. He told her he had no power to do that; the woman was free and could act her own pleasure.

Sarah had a mind to stay on, as her mistress had always treated her kindly, but Jim insisted on joining Sherman's train. Just before they left, one Saturday Campbell, who had been one of

Sarah's five husbands, and was the father of her child Anne, came and claimed Sarah. Jim fought and conquered him, thus winning Sarah and her children. They walked nearly a hundred miles, Sarah carrying Margery, a two-year-old child, in her arms. She kept the other children in front of her, for many lost their children.

After dinner of tea and crackers, which was our breakfast and supper also for nearly three weeks, we visited our neighbors. Their faces shone when we told them why we had come. They all seemed decent and sensible creatures.

We learn that there are ten thousand

negroes here. The officers and the teachers are the only white people allowed on the island, except the commissary, who is four miles away.

The negroes go to him once a month for rations. Sherman's plan is to have the negroes take care of themselves; they have planted corn, beans, and cotton, and are to repay the Government when their crops are gathered. This seems to be understood by all.

We walked down the road to a church, which bore marks of destruction similar to those of our house. The frame of the organ remains, the windows are gone, doors off their hinges, and pews mutilated, but we

decided that it would serve our purpose well as a school-house.

We have announced that we will
open school Monday. Many of the
older blacks ask if they are too old to
learn to read. They cannot come to
school during the day as it is planting
time, so we have promised to have an
evening school at the house twice a
week.

We have engaged Sarah, for five or
six dollars a month, to wash, iron, and
do the little cooking we shall have.

Her second son, Zack, about fourteen, is to wait upon us. He was
with Dr. Leavitt, at Fort Sumter, and
one day a horse on which he was riding was killed by a Union shell.

At the sutler's we found a man who is both baker and carpenter. He is to put locks or bolts on our doors, and to set some window glass.

All the negroes we have seen are industrious, and their cabins look neat. We found plum trees loaded with fruit all along the way, and plenty of black-berries.

MAY 13.

Mr. Blake came to see if he could be of service. He, with the aid of Jim, took our big packing-box and made us a table to eat from, and a bench to sit upon at meal time, so that we need not bring our chairs down from the bedrooms. Chairs are a great luxury.

In the afternoon, we walked to the "Mikell Place," two miles away, where live two teachers, also belonging to the Freedmen's Bureau, — Miss Kempton, from New Bedford, and Miss Stanton, from Framingham. Their house was large, dirty, and dilapidated. About a well in a large courtyard in front of the house, several blacks with tubs were doing their week's washing.

Returning, we met many people coming from the commissary with their rations. Some had sacks, others boxes or tubs on their heads. They asked if we had rations, and being told that we had not yet been supplied, they lowered their tubs and offered to give

us some of theirs. We thought them
very generous.

SUNDAY, MAY 14.

A beautiful day, though rather warm.
We started for church, but to our surprise met the congregation coming
away. There was to be a funeral at
a distance, and the minister had to
omit the church service. Later we
saw the procession, a long one. They
were singing a melancholy dirge as
they walked. As they passed, they
spoke to us, the men touching their
hats, and the women curtsying.

Seating ourselves on the steps of a
deserted house, we soon had a crowd
about us. One girl amused us — a

regular Topsy, who had come from
Georgia with Sherman. She examined our clothes, got behind Emily,
felt of her dress, and said, "Big plaits
in skirts are just coming into style."
The fashion had reached the South,
and all the ladies had been changing
their skirts.

Then catching sight of the "water-
fall" on my head, she was amazed,
and said, "Rebel ladies don't know
how to make them."

Monday, May 15.
The weather is much the same that
we have in June, cool mornings and
evenings, warm in the middle of the
day.

We opened school at nine o'clock, with fifteen scholars, nine boys, and six girls. Some were decently clad, others filthy and nearly naked. One or two knew their letters. None could read. We dismissed early, as the children seemed tired and we were decidedly weary.

On the way home we met the old woman who threw crockery at our windows the night of our arrival. She told us she was "great on religion," and read us a long sermon — how to live that we might die when called — and ended by saying she was "as poor as Job's turkey." When asked how poor that was, she said he had but one feather, and that all she had was on her back, and mighty little of that.

We have hired boys to collect and cure the gray moss for our bed-sacks. At any rate, it will be better than the bare boards, on which we are now lying.

MAY 16.

Passing a tumbled-down house on our way to school, we heard hammers, and going in, found some men making a coffin out of the boards. During school, we saw them back of the church digging the grave, hoeing out the dirt with their large cotton hoes (their only implement).

We had twenty-eight scholars. Two

of the new ones can read. This is pleasanter than teaching ABC. Two children, John and Eliza, came five miles to school. John was fourteen and a bright boy. He was nearly naked, and so filthy that I did not think I could have him near me, and advised him to go into the creek to bathe.

Every noon I take home with me a troop of children, to whom I give thread, needles, and pieces of cloth, that they may have their garments patched at home. We are trying to teach cleanliness as well as reading and spelling, but it is a tough job, for the poor creatures have lived so long in a filthy condition that they don't know what it is to be clean. Soon after we reached home, Eliza came running to tell us that her brother John had been drowned in the creek. He went in with several others, got beyond his depth and did not know how to swim. The tide, which was coming in, is very strong just at that point, and John was carried beyond the reach of those with him. It was a terrible shock to us, and I felt partly responsible.

Our dinner was excellent. We had hominy, brought by a man we met on the road one day, and one of our children caught some crabs, which Sarah boiled. We feel as if we had had a sumptuous feast — such a change from tea and crackers!

There is an open fireplace in Sarah's room, where she makes our tea in a small tin cup, which we brought from home, and boils hominy in — I don't know what, — nor do I ask. At night all the family (six children) stretch themselves on the floor in front of the fire, and so sleep. They have no bedding of any kind, neither chairs nor tables. They have a bowl, one plate, and one spoon. At meal-times they take turns in using these. They sit on the floor of the piazza; a portion is put into the bowl, — hominy or beans with a tiny bit of salt pork, — and they eat by turns. The children

27

are well behaved. George, the eldest boy, is religious and dull; Zack, our waiter boy, is a high-flier; Charlotte, quiet and not well; Ann, a pert piece, bright-eyed and devoted to us. Ben is a nice, chubby little fellow, who will go to school and can't keep awake. Ann flies at him every few minutes, and shakes him up. Margery, two years old, is a pretty little creature.

To-day I found a singular insect on my neck. We have been warned we should meet with such enemies, but this is the first of this kind. Woodticks we have already had, mosquitoes and fleas are yet to come.

May 17.

A very warm morning. We find our half-mile walk to school tiresome. A large school, sixty-six scholars, and rather unruly. Poor Emily is not adapted to deal with rough boys. I am obliged to go to her aid and, stamping my feet and shouting my commands, bring them to order. We are teaching the children the days of the week, the months, and also to count.

Mr. Blake visited the school, and we had a call also from the colored Baptist minister, who has a school somewhere on the island.

He asked to what denomination we belonged. He had never heard of Unitarians and asked what was our belief. We told him, and then he asked us to teach in his Sunday school, which we agreed to do in the fall when it is cooler.

Mr. Redpath has issued a mandate forbidding the reading of the Bible in school — no religious exercise except saying the Lord's Prayer.

John's body has been washed up by the tide and recovered.

MAY 18.

Mr. Blake made a blackboard for us, wasting several eggs and nearly all our ink before he succeeded.

Jim killed a snake, which he called a chicken snake, as they come where there are chickens. Our neighbors have many chickens so tame that they are in our house constantly. Last week a big rattlesnake was killed in our garden, and a huge black snake in our yard. We have seen only one, and that the children called a glass snake, for when struck it flew into many pieces all wriggling and alive. We see lizards everywhere.

Six new scholars. A woman came with a prayer-book, asking to be taught to read it. We told her we would teach her willingly, but it would be some time before she could read that. She was satisfied, and as she was leaving, put her hand under her apron and brought out two eggs — one she put in Emily's lap, the other in mine.

Our first rations came to-day, brought
by the men from headquarters. A
large box — a soap-box — with beans
at the bottom, covered by a piece of
dirty paper, then a layer of brown
sugar, and on top of all a bar of soap
and six candles. Some ground coffee
in a paper, a smaller bag with fat
bacon and salt pork, and a half barrel
of flour.

Emily came down and viewed the
lot, burst into tears and wished that
the grave we had seen hoed out at the
church was to lay her in. Poor Emily!
I was disheartened, but knew we must
make the best of it. We walked up to
the sutler's, who said he would take
all we did not want, and give us in

exchange from his stores. We got condensed milk, butter, cornmeal, and other things, and Sarah cooked us a royal supper. We felt better after a decent meal, and Emily concluded to live a while longer.

Later a woman came in suffering severe pain. We administered cayenne tea sweetened with brown sugar, and she was relieved.

The evening was delightfully cool. We had our first evening school for men and women on our piazza. It was well attended, all sitting on the floor and steps. One woman, who was much bent with rheumatism, and seemed very old, said she was "Mighty anxious to know something."

Late in the evening Dr. Mason
came to tell us that Jefferson Davis,
Stevens, and Clay had been taken
prisoners in Georgia and sent North.

MAY 19.

School went off very well — boys
less noisy. A man came in and sat
at the back of the church to listen to
our teaching, and the boys thought
we had engaged him to whip them if
they misbehaved. We have found out
that the boys are afraid of their fathers,
who are "Great on licking," so we shall
threaten to report them if they are
unruly.

The ivy round our house is beautiful; the lower part of the building is

covered. We have got the men to trim up the trees in our avenue, and to hoe out the road. On either side of our door are clove trees, full of fruit, and in the yard we have found a Cape Jessamine in full flower and a white Crêpe Myrtle. We are trying to get more sun on the house.

MAY 20, SATURDAY.

No school, and we devote the day to house-cleaning. We feel so much better for having more food. Crackers and tea are not strength-giving. Dr. Mason came in the large army wagon, bringing us from Beaufort a stove, tea-kettle, and coffee-pot. We cannot have our stove put up, as Jim, our Prime

Minister, is having toothache and cannot attend to matters. We already see a change in the appearance of our scholars. They are cleaner, and though wearing the same garments the rents are sewed up and patches are put on.

MAY 21.

Lieutenant Jenkins, who with Mrs. Webb had invited us to spend the day in the camp, came for us in his carriage. The three-mile drive was beautiful. We did not half appreciate it the day we came. The six officers, who were smoking on the piazza, gave us a cordial greeting.

At the end of a shady walk back of

36

the house are the fish and terrapin ponds. Around the fish pond is a broad carriage drive shaded by immense oak trees. A lovely grove of large trees beyond was approached by an avenue of tall laurels, planted so closely that they formed a thick hedge on either side, and met over our heads, shutting out completely the rays of the sun. At four o'clock we went out to see the dress parade of the colored soldiers.

MAY 23.

Nearly the whole school escorted us home to-day.

We sat on the piazza, and dealt out needles, thread, combs, and dresses from Mrs. Pillsbury's store.

One girl brought back a dress she had taken home, for "Ma says it don't fit, and she don't want it." It was rather large and rather short, but she was very dirty and ragged, and we told her she must keep it. Another girl promised to bring us a chicken if she could have a dress. We gave her one, and she soon came back with six eggs.

We live with hens, pigs, and quantities of rabbits, which the children have for pets. Occasionally, a rabbit is killed and eaten.

Jim has put up our stove; the pipe being too short for the chimney, he has put it out a window.

MAY 24.

It was one o'clock when school closed. We have so many grades that we cannot put them in classes, and it takes longer. The big boys are unruly. Emily is a good singer, and when the school is too much for us, we start singing, and that calms them down.

Several children came and demanded clothing as a right. A girl brought back a dress, saying it was "scant." She wanted a fuller skirt and a hoop-skirt.

MAY 25.

School was getting pretty unruly when a big man appeared to ask for "learning." The boys quieted down. I had threatened to get a man to help me whip the bad boys, and evidently they thought he had come for that purpose.

We paid Sarah her wages; the first money she ever earned or handled.

We found, growing in great quantities beside the road, the Passion flower, in full bloom.

Some men brought the dried moss for our beds. It is cured by soaking it five days in salt water, then drying it in the sun. It is jet black and very dry. We have paid Uncle Jack for it. Jim will pick it over, and fill our bed-sacks. We shall have soft beds to lie upon to-night.

Dr. Mason advises us to go to the bay soon. It will not be safe to stay on the island after the weather becomes hot. There is danger of fever.

SATURDAY, MAY 27.

No school. The morning being fine and the roar of the ocean plainly heard, we decided to drive to the bay. I cannot describe our conveyance. There were large spaces between the floor boards of the cart; both horses were skeletons, one large and the other small. The harness was of ropes and small cords, with twine for reins.

The road was much overgrown, flowers of all kinds lined the way, and turkey buzzards were sitting in solemn conference. Within a quarter of a mile of Edingsville — as the bay is called — we reached a creek, which we crossed on a flat-bottomed raft and walked to the long row of houses on the beach. Once this was a famous summer resort, and some of the houses are very pretty. The beach is broad and hard, and the surf was grand. We went to several houses, looking for one that suited us for a summer home.

Meeting Mr. Everett and the two ladies, they invited us to share with them a pleasant house they had found. We will decide later.

After we had gone to bed we heard a clatter of horses' feet, and Dr. Mason and Captain Crissy appeared with our mail. Fatigue and headaches were forgotten; we sat up half the night reading our letters and talking of home.

MAY 28.

The army wagon brought our long-delayed and much-needed bedsteads. With them and our moss beds we shall not want to get up at five every morning. We have lain on the bare floor nearly three weeks.

Our shutters and blinds have been mended, and we sent to Charleston for glass for the windows.

Uncle Jack's pig was stolen last night, the second within a few weeks. He says he is going to Charleston to consult a fortune-teller to find out the thief. We advise him to stay at home and to watch for the guilty person.

May 29.

Walker has made us a chair and table, for which we paid a good price. Some coarse straw hats, suitable only for bathing, cost us a dollar and a half apiece.

In our walk this afternoon, we saw a man and woman who seemed well-informed. They hope to prove to the "Secesh" that colored folks can work and accomplish something without masters or overseers; for it has always been said that "Niggers wouldn't work unless compelled." The woman's name is Lydia Polite. She gave us cucumbers and peanuts.

We asked another woman if she is contented. She answered, "God bless you, I reckon I am — I heard for a long time of war and the coming of the Yankees, and I spects my bones be white before I see that time, but I did live to see them, bress de Lord." She said she had raised "Ten head of childen." Three little ones were with her.

Mr. Everett brought us some school books, for which we are thankful.

MAY 31.

We walked across the fields to the Baptist Church, where the colored minister has his school. He came to meet us — said his mother was upstairs sick with smallpox, so we only went through the lower floor, and out the back door into the pretty garden. In the evening the family sang for us, "Heaven's bell ringing — won't turn back heaven's bell ringing for believers." Another was, "Sister, you come too late, the Devil been and shut the gate and carried off the keys"; then "Don't judge me, Lord, O Lord — don't be offended," and "Thar's rejoicing ober yander"; "Let me go, Jacob will not let me go," this repeated over and over, and "Oh, my Lord, help us."

Diary in Dixie

June 1.

President's Fast — no school. Zack is in trouble again; he did not go to church as ordered. We have told Sarah we cannot have so much "licking"; it is too much for our nerves, to say nothing of Zack's back.

Mr. Everett arrived, sick. We have cleared out one of our back rooms making it as comfortable as possible, and have put it at his disposal. He has overworked, and walked too much in the hot sun.

A rattlesnake was killed in the yard. It had wound itself round a hen, that was sitting on her nest under a laurel.

At the store we met the captain of the little boat that brought us to the island, and the boat agent. They are surprised that we have stayed, thought we were "too fine." As our rations seem to have been overlooked, they offered to get them for us.

Mrs. Pillsbury sent us a bag of rice, and we have been living on that, with the few eggs and vegetables we could get.

JUNE 2.

Mr. Everett is quite sick. We sent to the commissary for the Government doctor, who had gone to Beaufort. Then we sent to headquarters for Dr. Mason. He says Mr. Everett has typhoid symptoms.

At school there were seventy schol-

48

ars, who behaved pretty well. A girl came just recovering from smallpox. She was indignant when we sent her away, but we pacified her by telling her she could come back in a few weeks. Going up to our bedroom we met on the stairs a rattlesnake. We screamed lustily, and Uncle Jack, Jim, George, and Zack appeared. I jumped over it, and it fell through the balusters to the hall, where the men killed it. We find in our room many holes where it could have come up in the walls from the cellar. To-morrow we shall paper our walls with news-papers.

JUNE 3.

Our regular cleaning day. Phœbe came to scour the floors. She was much pleased with a pink calico apron I made for her. Uncle Jack brought us a ripe fig. Never saw one before. We shall have plenty if the children don't steal all that are on the tree.

Mr. Everett has been telling us the amount of rations the Government allows each person. It is ample, and we are sure we have never had our full allowance.

We have papered part of our chamber with newspapers, covering the places where the plastering is broken, where the snake may have come up.

Little Ben went to walk with us.

Passing Sandy's house, he said, "When Sandy no at school, me make no piece of noise." Passed the evening listening to George and Zack. Their owner rented them out to a hotel-keeper in Sumterville. They were worked day and night, never going to bed until after one o'clock, and getting up at four to go to the station on arrival of trains. Sundays they were allowed one hour to go home, three miles away, for clean clothes. The hotel-keeper paid their master twenty dollars a month for each.

SUNDAY, JUNE 4.

No churchgoing — too warm, and the walk too long for Sundays, as we

51

are obliged to take it every week-day. We seated ourselves on the piazza to write letters. Soon a crowd of children were around us, all wanting books, and before we knew it we were teaching school. George and Zack came with the others. George is patient and promising. We are surprised at the ease with which he acquires the sound of words. He teaches his father after leaving us.

Dr. Mason does not think Mr. Everett will be sick long. He needs rest and nourishing food.

The captain of the *Hudson* offered to get our rations in the city. We gave him our bags and trust they will be returned well filled. At bedtime

we heard a boat whistle. We may
have letters to-morrow.

JUNE 6.

The store-keeper brought two stools
for our use in school; we found it so
hard to stand all the time. At eleven,
Mr. Blake brought our letters, papers
and rations. Emily left for home.
Four letters for me, and sixty scholars
to attend to before I could open them!
We forgot our dinner and spent the
afternoon reading each other's letters
and talking of home. The rations
were ample; we made exchanges at
the store.

JUNE 7.

Coming home I met Lieutenant Jenkins, who told me twenty rebels had been caught on the island. They landed at a place, three or four miles away, called Upper Landing. The object of their coming is not known.

JUNE 9.

School over for the week. Very, very hot weather. Emily has much headache from the long walk and exposure to the sun. School and waiting on Mr. Everett take so much time that I cannot write. He is better, but not able to leave his room. Mr. Blake, who came to see him, was surprised and delighted with our school; he said

Miss K.'s and Miss S.'s school bore no comparison, — and *they* "certified" schoolma'ams! We are quite elated. Our books number a hundred and forty scholars, and from sixty to seventy are in daily attendance. Our evening school on the piazza is well attended, and we enjoy our labors. All are respectful and eager to learn. We notice that all the children and grown-ups also hold their books sidewise; when we asked why, a man answered "We wish to learn to read on all sides."

JUNE 10.

Phœbe came to wash the floors, and Julia, the windows. I gave the latter a pink calico apron, and Phœbe some flour and coffee, which satisfied her. She said she would give herself to us every Saturday. To Uncle Jack, who cleaned up the yard, I gave a hat. He was tickled, never having owned a covering for his head before. We had a good dinner, — some ham, salad of lettuce, which Henry's grandmother sent us, and some biscuits without butter. Dr. Mason took supper with us. He was much amused with our rooms neatly papered with Springfield and New York papers.

SUNDAY, JUNE 11.

Hottest morning we have had — not a breath of air. Dr. Mason advises us to leave the island as soon as possible — not safe for us to stay much longer. A woman who brought some cucumbers said she would make any sacrifice to serve us, who were doing so much to teach her children, who knew nothing but how to handle a hoe. George killed another rattlesnake under the plum tree, — they are after the figs — horrid creatures!

JUNE 12.

Three colored clergymen visited our school. They told the scholars to be neat and clean, and to heed all that was taught them.

JUNE 13 AND 14.

Intolerably hot days — rather cooler at night. Had a very large school, one hundred and one scholars — too many — cannot keep order with so many. I am well worn out before noon with shouting and stamping, for I am obliged to help Emily when she gets into difficulty. We stayed after school closed with three unruly boys, rough and tough customers, who confessed that they liked to tease us; but they were ashamed and promised to do better in the future.

Captain Storrs called. He told us there were five guerrillas at camp; they had been caught on the island, but there is no evidence to convict them and they will probably be set at liberty.

JUNE 15.

Hot, hotter, hottest! Impossible to go up to the church for school. The children came down to see why we did not appear. We kept them and had school on the piazza; Emily there, and I down in the yard.

Mr. Blake brought whisky and remedies for Mr. Everett. He went to Beaufort for them, and nearly lost his life coming back. A storm arose, and the high wind blew their little boat thirty miles out to sea; if he had not had a small compass, he could not have got back. Mr. Blake gave us liberty to stop teaching when we like, and we have decided, as it is so fearfully hot and Emily's head troubles her so

much, to have school in our house
until we can go to the bay for our
vacation. Mr. Blake has left his poor,
half-starved white horse for Mr. Everett
to ride to his home. It is in our shed,
tormented by mosquitoes and flies.

JUNE 16.

Jim and Uncle Jerry have cleared
out our big front room and arranged
some boards on blocks for seats for the
older children. The little ones can sit
on the floor. Fifty came this morning.
They are to bring stools — as many
as have them — so we shall get on well.

Mr. Everett bade us farewell, riding
off on his white beast; he seemed
pretty weak. Mr. Redpath writes that

we are to report to Mr. Pillsbury, as he himself goes North on the next steamer, and advises us to close our school. All the Charleston schools are closed, as there is much sickness; one northern teacher having died. He thinks we had better go North for our vacation. We cannot do that, for we should never return.

If our friends at home could only see our flowers! Cloth of gold roses and lovely Cape Jessamines. The evening was pleasant; the children sang to us and we told them stories, — Red Riding Hood, etc. They had never listened before to stories of any kind, and were most attentive.

JUNE 18.

Still close and hot. A shower at noon with lightning and terrible thunder, as we never heard it before. Spent the day writing letters home and had Sunday school in the evening.

JUNE 19.

We like the new school arrangement, for we do not get so warm, can wear loose sacks, and can spare our lungs.

When we feel tired, we sing, which they all enjoy. They particularly delight in singing "Hang Jeff Davis to a sour apple tree."

The children told us some of their experiences in slave life. One boy,

62

Tom, showed us deep scars on his arms; said they were from severe whippings. When about eight years old, he rode a horse to a distant place, and lost the colt that was following; and of course was whipped. Many of the negroes were born on the island, and are glad to get back to their old homes.

JUNE 20 AND 21.

Rain for two days. No children came, and we enjoyed the holiday. Heard a boat whistle, but the rain will prevent our sending the boys to camp for our letters. Sarah came to our room after dinner, and we had a nice talk. She is very quiet and never

63

talks of her experiences unless questioned; then she speaks with reluctance and much feeling. She says "It's time slaves were free, they've suffered enough. Only Jesus knows what they've endured." The song, "Nobody knows but Jesus," tells the story. She said no slave mother could have her children after they were old enough to be of use; they were sold or hired out. She had often seen her children abused — punished severely for small faults.

She had prayed and prayed that one child — her oldest — might die. The girl was not very strong, and had the care of a fretful baby, when little more than a baby herself. At last God heard her prayer, and her child died. No one could tell how thankful she was. Talk of the happiness of slaves! None were ever happy. They became hardened to their lot and were cheerful, but mothers were always anxious, dreading separation from their children.

Walter, one of our scholars, told us that he saw a box addressed to us on the Charleston boat. He sat on it all the way. What news! probably it is on the wharf soaking in this rain.

JUNE 22.

Rain still coming down in torrents, but we must have our box, so we started off some boys with umbrellas

65

to find out about it and bring our letters.
They brought a big packet of letters,
and the camp wagon brought our box
from home, and three barrels from
the Pillsburys in Charleston. We
worked hard all the evening unpack-
ing and looking over our treasures.
Oh! such gingerbread was never before
made and eaten. We did not care
for supper. Phœbe was transformed
by her new dress. Uncle Jack says
"She will be getting a new man now
she is so fine." Uncle Jack and Jim
are resplendent in new coats and
trousers. Zack is a picture in a
Zouave suit of Jack King's.

Diary in Dixie

JUNE 23 AND 24.

The rain continues and everything is damp and sticky. The roof leaks badly and our chamber is in a sad state. George and Watson arrived early, having heard of our box of clothing. They will mend the roof, and we shall pay them with clothing. Watson demanded a whole suit. We thought that a large order, but found we could fill it, even to the hat and boots. We first dressed up our immediate family, Sarah and the children. Ann is fine in a blue Garibaldi of Jeannie G.'s, and Abby in white pantalettes and a blue poplin, once Jeannie's. George wears a suit of Henry Freeman's and Fred Harris's hat.

Mr. Blake came to say good-by for two months.

SUNDAY, JUNE 25.

The sun came out and we had Sunday school in the school-room. I do the preaching and Emily attends to the singing. She is highly amused at my teachings. What surprises me is that they know so little of the life of Christ; not knowing even of his birth, but they all are familiar with his sayings. They all believe in a hell! I asked the children whom they love best. Some answered "God"; Zack said, "Ma; she loves me and feeds me." After school, George came and reproved me for telling stories to the children on Sunday. He considers it sinful.

Lydia Polite came to tell us that her baby had died. She is a very good, sensible woman.

JUNE 26.

Eighty children, and not enough room for them. We heard the alphabet classes and turned them out in the yard to play. A thunder shower freshened the air so we could walk to the store to inquire how we could get to the bay.

Since the boxes of clothing came, we have been besieged by half the island. Some, whom we do not know, and who live miles away, demand clothing and say they have a right to it. I have called Uncle Jack to the rescue. He knows how to deal with them, and explains that the clothing does not come from the Government, and that they must pay for it with vegetables, eggs, chickens, or whatever they can bring in exchange. Before we were up this morning, Phœbe appeared with a live rooster some one had brought. She said she would make a pen for it, as we were provided with food for the day. Before night two more were brought. Soon we shall have a rooster house.

A girl came to school with traces of smallpox on her face. When questioned, she said her baby had died recently. We sent her off, indignant that she came, and she was equally indignant that she was dismissed.

Uncle Jack has heard of a man who owns a horse and cart, and we have told him to find out what day he will take us to the bay. Uncle Jack says we have "Done spile the people here." Well! we can soon un-spile them.

JUNE 28.

Clear, and a refreshing west wind. We had a sumptuous dinner, — fried chicken, new potatoes, green corn, and watermelons for dessert. Sounds well, our *menu*, but the corn was so dry it could not be eaten. Phœbe brought the live chicken in her arms "For

71

Missis' dinner, Mum." The potatoes came from a man who brought a cracked looking-glass and asked for a gun in exchange. We took the glass and gave him coat, trousers, and a hat. The holes in our bedroom were filled with plaster made of mud and dried moss.

JUNE 30.

We told the children when we dismissed them, that this is the last day of school, but as we do not mean to leave the island immediately, we will teach a few if they will come to us.

JULY 2.

A visit from a Mr. Curtis who keeps a store at Peters Point, seven miles from here. He brought the news that the soldiers stationed here are ordered to leave at once for Beaufort, to join the rest of the regiment. We are troubled because we depend upon them for our mail and packages. All the afternoon we wrote, that our letters might be ready for to-night's steamer. George, Zack, and Uncle Jack took them to the landing and gave them into the hands of Captain Storrs, who sent us a good-by.

JULY 3.

It is a great relief to have no school. Got out the materials sent from home and cut and fitted our bathing suits.

We took a walk through the fields, and saw Lydia Polite hoeing her cotton, which looks well, full of blossoms. Next we saw our friends, Jerry and Louisa Pious, with the children, Abby and Ellen. They were setting out slips of the sweet potato vine. Abby handled the hoe as well as a man. The baby, on its back between the ridges was happy.

From a row of cabins that we passed many of our scholars ran out to meet us; their nakedness was barely covered, but we are used to that. They asked us to go into their homes, which were miserable, dark, and dirty. Another friend showed us a cotton-gin soon to be put in order and worked. We walked by a rice field; the blades were just above the ground, fresh and green.

We had a call from Mr. Everett, who is quite well again. He offered to go down to the bay to select a house for us; we have agreed to go next week if we can find a conveyance.

JULY 4.

Independence Day. Perfect quiet reigns. We imagine we hear the cannon and firecrackers at home. It is so very warm that we have no life, and lay on the bed all the morning. James Russell offered us his horse and cart for the day for two dollars and a half.

JULY 5.

Up early. James Russell came with horse and cart, and at nine we set off with Zack, Ben, and our luncheon. The cart is what we call a dump-cart. We seated ourselves in the middle to balance, but when the horse went faster than a walk we were so thrown about that we had to sit on the floor. The harness was of rope — mostly twine; the shafts fell to the ground every few minutes, and Zack, who drove, was on the continual jump to replace them. We were nearly two hours going the three miles. When we reached the creek back of the bay, the bridge was gone, but the tide being low we were able to cross. Such a delicious cool breeze welcomed us, and such a beautiful, broad, hard beach. We enjoyed the day, eating lunch on the piazza of one of the most imposing houses. We visited a dozen or more houses, looking for one suitable for our summer abode. The only one that pleased us is that selected by Mr. Everett for himself and the other teachers; as it is large enough to accommodate us all, we shall ask our friends to let us have one half the house.

Because of the tide we had to wait until after sunset, starting for home about seven o'clock. Our horse refused to enter the creek; one of the men led him in, the water being only a little above the man's knees. Half

way across, the horse stopped and refused to move. Suddenly he started
down the creek and lay down, the
water nearly covering the cart. I
wanted to jump out, but Emily held
on to my dress. The men came out
and carried us over to the land, then
unharnessed the horse and led him
back.

The fright and lateness of the hour
(for our three miles drive was through
thick woods) decided us to remain all
night on the beach. We went back to
the piazza; Zack and Ben were soon
asleep; Emily and I were not so fortunate. We were heated by our long
walk, and disturbed in mind. The
night was glorious. A bright moon

made it as light as day. We walked
the beach and watched the waves.

JULY 6.

A cool and refreshing morning after
our uneasy night. The water's edge
is only a few feet from the house. All
the houses, sixty or more, are built
close down on the beach. After we
made our toilets, Zack built a fire and
boiled some eggs. Before we had
eaten them, we heard voices, and soon
Jim and Uncle Jack appeared. All
the people in our yard had been greatly
worried and unable to sleep, fearing
we had been drowned. At daybreak,
Sarah had sent Jim and Uncle Jack
in search of us. Soon George arrived

He could not wait for the others to return. We had a fine escort as we went back to the place where we had left the horse and cart. A little higher up the creek was a raft on which we crossed.

JULY 7.

Robert came to borrow money to buy a "shoat." Three dollars for the pig and "a little more," if we could spare it. As Rhoda, his woman, is to work for us this summer, we lent him five dollars.

JULY 9.

Phœbe said Louisa was going to have some friends for tea — would we

contribute the sugar? They were going to have a Praise Meeting in the
yard, but Jim asked permission to
have it on the back piazza if it would
not disturb us. We consented, and
told him we should like to be present.
An Elder who could read, led the singing. George held for him a lighted
candle, which we supplied. The leader
read one or two lines from the hymn-
book; then they all sang, each man for
himself. After the singing, the Elder
prayed. He asked the blessed Lord
to raise the window curtains this blessed
night and let the poor sinners look in,
and if it was the blessed Lord's will,
would he this blessed evening send
down his angels with a hammer and

knife and knock at every sinner's heart, for many there are this blessed evening, weeping and tearing their hair and searching for religion, and not knowing how to get it. They sang again, then the sisters walked round in a circle with short, quick steps, swinging their arms and singing, "Oh! Lord, don't be offended. Oh! Lord, don't judge me hard," and much more of the same strain. They kept this up a long time; the meeting lasted till long after midnight. One song was "Sister, you come too late, the Devil came and shut the gate and carried home the keys." Another, "When Gabriel blow his horn for Massa Jesus would he please blow a little louder?"

Diary in Dixie

JULY 10.

Packed more of our belongings and finished the bathing suits. I put mine on and went into the yard, which greatly amused the children, who had never seen such a rig.

JULY 11.

When the man came with his wagon, we doubted if the horses could carry us three miles, they were such skeletons, and the man said they could not drag a heavy load. We put in our most desirable articles and started the load off about ten o'clock, Jim and Uncle Jack walking. Cuffee came to sell watermelons in a nice cart, with a seat and a back to it, and we offered him two dollars to take us to the bay. We waited for Jim to get back because we were determined to have all our possessions moved before night. He did not get here until three o'clock because the horses could not pull the load through the sand, and the trunks and everything had to be "toted" on the men's heads across the creek and up the beach to the house. Then another load was put on the cart, and we packed ourselves and what we most needed into Cuffee's wagon and started. Cuffee walked. Emily held the strings, and I, the tin pail, box, etc.

They carried the things across a broken bridge, a shorter way than by the ford; and we were glad to be in our summer home by the sea.

EDISTO BAY, JULY 12.

A beautiful morning, fresh and cool. Our friends soon took their departure for the island. We were sorry to part with them.

Soon some soldiers appeared, inquiring for the house which is to be occupied by Mr. Alden, the Government Superintendent of Edisto Island, who is to arrive to-day.

JULY 13.

Such a morning and such surf never were known. New life has been given us. We ought to have come here a month ago. We were surprised this morning by receiving a quart of new milk from Mr. Alden's house, with the request that we send for it every morning. Such luxury — the first milk we have seen since leaving Charleston. As for bread, we have forgotten how it looks. We have corn-meal (white), which stirred up with water and an egg makes a very nice cake.

JULY 15.

Received a letter from Mr. Blake in Beaufort, saying that the Government has stopped our rations, and that we must either supply ourselves, or the society, by which we are employed, must do so. He advised us to go north, but we have decided to remain for the summer, at least; it is too warm now to take the long journey.

Our house is pleasant and comfortable, though minus a front door and some of the windows. We have taken two lower rooms; one looking on the water, for our sleeping and living-room, and the other for the dining-room. The kitchen is across the yard, which is deep with sand, washed up by the creek. At high tide we are wholly surrounded by water.

Besides Rhoda and "her man," Robert, we have George, who sleeps across the threshold where the door should be; so we feel safe.

We have called upon Mr. Alden, who has horses, servants, and some colored soldiers, and he has promised to bring our mail from the landing, seven miles away. This is a great relief.

We find the bathing delightful, and ventured out quite far, until Robert caught a shark in shore.

Jim has been down, bringing little Ben for a visit. I have dressed him in a suit of underwear which came in a barrel of clothing from the "Church of the Disciples" (Boston). He sleeps on the floor beside my bed. One night, as he hung over my chair, he was uneasy, and I asked what troubled him. He whispered, "Is the reason

88

you don't kiss me 'cause I'm black?"
I took him into my lap and held him
till he slept.

Miss Kempton and Miss Stanton
will occupy two rooms of this house.
They will do their own cooking and
will not interfere with us.

We have only two chairs — mine,
a steamer chair; Emily's, a pretty
straight-backed one; very tiresome to
sit in long at a time; we often exchange
and oftener stretch ourselves on the
floor to rest. Our great need is drink-
ing water. There is an open cistern
back of the house; this we used till a
party of our colored visitors in a frolic
threw their hats into it. A burly old
darky waded in and fished them out,

and since then we have used watermelons to quench our thirst. A coat, vest, or hat in exchange will get us a plenty. We keep a pile on the floor of our dining-room, and cut one when thirsty.

Our food is getting low. We are often hungry. Government flour is full of weevils, little bugs, that baking does not kill. We pick out the wriggling creatures and eat the bread dipped in molasses, but soon we shall have eggs and vegetables.

A child has been born to Sarah. She has not named it yet, as it is considered bad luck to give a name to a child before it is a month old. She means to call her Mary Emily.

Diary in Dixie

We carried some clothing to our namesake, a light-colored individual with a large head of wool, and found poor Sarah in great trouble. We knew that Zack and Marjorie had been sick with fever, and now Jim is very ill.

The bill from the store made to "Mrs. Mary teacher," is a curiosity.

Mr. Everett has astonished us all. He has received from the society in Boston one hundred dollars for two months' rations for the five teachers on Edisto.

The blacks at the landing are dissatisfied. There is trouble about their rations, and they complain that Willis,

the man in charge, is cruel. He says
he has acted under Mr. Alden's orders,
and so they are angry with him too.
There are some three hundred of them.
Several were put under guard Saturday, and the trial comes Monday. We
are anxious, but Mr. Alden has no
fears.

On Sunday Mr. Alden went to the
two churches and talked to the people,
telling them "the law." The women
were turned out of church before the
men began to talk.

When Jim was sick, Sarah sent her
baby to the neighbors to be cared for,
and devoted herself to the sick ones.
We did everything in our power, giving

money and other things to make them comfortable. Jim died the twelfth of September. Sarah had succumbed to the same disease, and two weeks later she died. The last time I saw her, she asked me to take her seven children north to my "plantation." I promised to do all I could.

We told Judy, who had taken the baby, that we would clothe it and pay her for its care, but she got tired of the child, and one day left it at our house and slipped away. Rhoda begged me to keep it and let her care for it, but I declined, knowing Mistress Rhoda and myself too well to enter into such a partnership. One of our neighbors, a young woman, took it for a time.

We consulted Mr. Alden about the children. George was old enough to take care of himself. Zack was given to a woman, who promised to treat him as her own. The younger children and baby were sent, several weeks later, to the Charleston orphan asylum.

Mary Emily did not live long, nor did Charlotte, who was a sickly little girl. Poor little Ben, the most affectionate of them all, refused to eat, and died of homesickness the next winter.

My sister, who came down to visit us, carried Ann, aged seven, and another little girl, Maggie Murphy, home with her. They have lived in Springfield ever since. Both are capable women. After we went north I sent for George and Zack, that they might work on our place, but they were so well employed at the Phosphate Works that we thought they would be happier if left among their own people.

We gave the stewardess of one of the New York boats money to bring little Marjorie to us, but when my brother-in-law went to the boat to get her, he was told that she was dying.

In October Mr. Alden was told to bring the people together that General Howard might talk to them about their future. On the nineteenth a cavalcade of twenty negroes, mounted on horses and mules of all kinds and sizes rushed down to the landing, and formed two lines, through which General Saxton and General Howard, with the other gentlemen, passed, receiving the horsemen's salute.

The church was crowded. General Howard, in simple words, said that he, being their friend, had been sent by the President to tell them that the owners of the land, their old masters, had been pardoned, and their plantations were to be given back to them; that they wanted to come back to cultivate the land, and would hire the blacks to work for them.

At first the people could not understand, but as the meaning struck them, that they must give up their little homes and gardens, and work again

for others, there was a general mur-
mur of dissatisfaction. General Howard's task grew more painful. He
begged them to lay aside their bitter
feelings, and to become reconciled to
their old masters. We heard mur-
murs of "No, never." "Can't do it."
General Howard proposed that three
men be chosen to represent the people,
to consult and report to him.

Meantime they were asked to sing,
and burst forth with "Nobody knows
the trouble I see," and "Wandering
in the wilderness of sorrow and gloom."
Two of the largest owners came down
with General Howard. Many of their
old slaves were in the church. It was
touching to see them saying "How dy"

to each other. The gentlemen also felt it. Tears were in their eyes. One of them made a long address.

Still the negroes would not trust them or their promises, declaring that they never could work again "for the Secesh." One said "It was very distressful." Another that he could forgive his old master, as he hoped to be forgiven, but he had lived all his life with a basket over his head, and now that it had been taken off and air and sunlight had come to him, he could not consent to have the basket over him again. It was a hard day for them, poor creatures.

The committee came back after some time, saying they could come to no decision, they were too much shaken to see things clearly.

A few days later, they drew up the following petition to the President:

DEAR PRESIDENT JOHNSON
OF THE UNITED STATES

Wee the freedmen of South Carlina wish to adress you with a few lines Conserning the sad feelings that is now resting upon our minds wee pray that god may guive you helth & good spirets that when you receive theas few notasis that you may receive them as the father did the prodical son wee have for the last four yars ben studing with justis and the best of our ability what step wee should

take to become a peple: wee have
lernt to respect all Just Causes that
ever came from the union.

"Mag genrl howard has paid the
freedmen of South Carlinah a visit &
caled a meating on Edisto Island South
Carliner in the Centrel part of the
island at the priskple Church thair hee
beutifly addressed the freedmen of
this island after his adress a grate
many of the peple understanding what
was said they got aroused & awoke to
perfict sense to stody for them Selves
what part of this law would rest against
us, wee said in rafarence to what he
said that nothing did apier at that time
to bee very opressing upon us but the
one thing that is wee freedmen should

work for wages for our former oners or eny other man president Johnson of u st I do say . . . man that have stud upon the feal of battle & have shot there master & sons now Going to ask ether one for bread or for shelter or Comfortable for his wife & children sunch a thing the u st should not aught to Expect a man (to do) . . ."

Continuing, they said: "the King of south Carolina ask the Privalage to have the stage that he might a Dress the ordenence [audience] of the freed-men. . . ."

This was the beginning of a scorching arraignment of the "old master," who had spoken at the meeting, who pretended to "such a fealing to Comply with the best order & also what was the best for the freedmen. . . ." "Here is Plenty Whidow & Fatherles that have serve you as slave now losen a home," and they beg that you "give Each one of them a acres & a ½ to a family as you has the labers & the Profet of there Yearly [early] Youth." And when "the Questin was asked him by General Howard, what would it sell your lan for a acres his anser the I would not take a hunderd $100 of a acres that is a part of his union fealing so then we therefore lose fate [faith] in this southern Gentelman" And then they beseech "the wise president that sets on his seat" to give them "a Chance to Recover out of this

trubble," . . . "these 3 Committee
has Pleg the Trouth to you dis day.
Oct. 25 1865."

All of us at headquarters were invited to dine on Christmas with Captain and Mrs. Towles, and their friends
on Wadmelaw Island. It was a foggy
morning, and we were not in the best
of spirits. Four of the soldiers rowed
us in a pontoon. The dinner of wild
turkey, etc., was excellent. The ladies
who were asked to meet us, and whom
we liked, had been sent out by the
Philadelphia Society.

Captain Towles had got a fiddle and
an old negro to play it, and insisted
upon our dancing, because it was

Christmas and we must be merry. It was bad music and worse dancing, but we danced ourselves into a great heat and great good spirits.

At seven we started for home, thinking an hour's rowing would bring us to Edisto. The night was lovely, a clear moonlight, and the tide in our favor. Soon we were in a dense fog, and it was difficult for the gentlemen to know where and when to turn to find the various creeks leading to Edisto. We were weary and uncomfortable, in fact lost, and at one o'clock, when the moon had set and we were in darkness, Captain Bacheller gave the order to land. We went ashore through deep mud, climbed a steep bank and found ourselves under some trees on what seemed to be an uninhabited island. The soldiers made a big camp-fire, and we lay down upon rubber blankets, a log covered with pine boughs and moss as a pillow. We were aroused by voices of men, who with their dogs had been hunting coons. To our surprise we learned from them that we were still on Wadmelaw Island. They told us how to get home. We slept once more and at six o'clock set off on the waters again, the fog being still very thick.

Again it was all a mystery and we proceeded much in the way of the night before, when suddenly we heard the drums at headquarters.

As we stepped upon the landing a note from Mr. Alden was given to Captain Bacheller with "Sad news" written upon it. He hurriedly opened the letter, and told us that our friends, Miss Kempton, Miss Stanton, and their friend, Mr. J. P. Blake, had been drowned in St. Pierre Creek. We were stunned, but drove immediately to their home, the Middleton Place.

They had been to see some friends two miles down the creek, and had nearly reached the landing on their return, when screams were heard; the boat, which was small and unseaworthy, had been overturned, and they were in the water. Mr. Blake was lame and unable to swim, and the

106

young women could not. A boat was quickly put out, but only the hats and cloaks of the girls were found floating near the spot.

Miss Kempton's body was recovered the next day. She was buried in the graveyard, back of the Congregational Church. Captain Bacheller read the service. All her school children came to look upon her, and walked to the churchyard singing as they went. Two of our hymns were also sung. Three weeks afterwards, Miss Stanton's body was brought back by the sea, and she was buried beside Ellen. Stones to mark the graves were sent down by their own people.

When we broke up the pleasant summer home in October, we established ourselves at the beautiful Seabrook place, which had been headquarters when we first came. We were much more comfortable than we had been in our first home. To be sure, the roof leaked and we were in danger of being drowned out, but we had become used to that. The windows were unglazed, except in those rooms in actual use. There were disturbing sounds in the garret where, upon investigation, we saw bones of birds and rats and heard unearthly spittings and hissings from behind a board. We thought these were made by "'possums," but later, when a pretty white owl was caught in the garret, and several flew past our window to the top of the house, we concluded that it was owls and not "'possums" that we heard at dead of night.

The school was in a building once used as a billiard room, which accommodated a large number of pupils. We often had a hundred and twenty, and when word went forth that supplies had come, the number increased. Indeed, it was so crowded that we told the men and women they must stay away to leave space for the children, as we considered teaching them more important. They left in high dudgeon. Our work was easier because the children were of a better class and had had some instruction.

When we made out the school report to send to Boston, we were surprised that out of the hundred, only three children knew their age, nor had they the slightest idea of it; one large boy told me he was "Three months old." The next day many of them brought pieces of wood or bits of paper with straight marks made on them to show how many years they had lived. One boy brought a family record written in a small book.

A false report having been circulated in Charleston, that the negroes on Edisto were in a state of insurrection, General Beecher sent here early in

December eighty colored soldiers with two (white) officers. We helped the gentlemen to start their mess, and the soldiers were a help to us in many ways.

We had been inconvenienced by the lack of a chimney in the schoolhouse. One day when, choking with smoke, we asked the children if some of their fathers could not come and fix the stove, they began, "I haven't any father" — "I live with Aunty," and so on. We were surprised to learn how orphaned our school was. Eight of Captain Bacheller's men built a chimney for us. In return we gave each of them a book, which pleased them. They were fine-looking fellows and all of them could read.

On New Year's day we went to the dinner given by the Captain to the soldiers. Their mess-room, the old storehouse of the plantation, was decorated with pine boughs and gray moss. The men spoke pieces, which they had committed to memory for the first time in their lives, and one, who two years ago did not know his letters, read the Emancipation Proclamation.

In January smallpox broke out among the soldiers quartered on our place. Many of our scholars took it, and we closed the school for five weeks. We escaped, although in continual danger, for the negroes, even when repulsively sick, were so eager for our gifts of clothing that they forced their way to our very bedrooms, and our carryall, drawn by men, was used to carry the patients to the improvised hospital. Several of our earliest friends on the Whaley place died. When on Monday, February twenty-sixth, we began school again, we had thirteen pupils. One of them, when asked if there was smallpox at her plantation, answered, "No, the last one died Saturday." On the third day one hundred children had come back.

Twice we had to go to Charleston. Several steamers touched at Edisto, but we sailed generally on the *John Adams*, a Boston ferry-boat, which the fortunes of war had brought to these strange waters. Both times we were detained coming back; once by fog and once by nightfall, which made navigation unsafe because of the obstructions placed in the river during the war by the Confederates. Anchored out at sea, in an East Boston ferry-boat, literally crammed with blacks, pigs, poultry, and furniture, was, to say the least, uncomfortable. The novelty of these visits was meat, which was a food unknown for months at a time at Edisto; the pleasure was in meeting Mrs. Pillsbury, who was always the same dear, kind lady. They had moved from their beautiful house to one that was dark and disagreeable.

Diary in Dixie

A (government) horse was sent to Emily; we had the carryall and a buggy which came from home. We were altogether so comfortable that we invited my sister Elizabeth, my friend Mrs. French, and Emily's sister and her husband to visit us. They came in February; helped us with our school and criticised our housekeeping.

Robert and Rhoda had come with us from the bay. Rhoda was not the best of cooks, and now that she was "Striving for religion," she and Robert had to go to so many "Shouts" and dances that we moved them into the basement, so that they might not disturb us by their late hours.

Perhaps this "Striving" was the

cause of her erratic cooking. We ate in silence the dried beef which she fried for breakfast, only wondering why the bacon was so queer.

Our friends, knowing that Emily was unusually fastidious, were surprised that we could live "In such a shiftless way." They said they "Would have things decent and the food properly cooked." We offered them the privilege of employing their New England energy in keeping house for us. One day was enough. At the end of it I asked my friend where she had been all day? "In the kitchen, holding up the stovepipe so that Lizzie could bake!"

They taught the alphabet to the

little children who had forgotten it during the smallpox vacation, and they clothed the older ones, who went from the school to the house in squads of four or five, coming back completely metamorphosed, their mouths stretched from ear to ear with delight.

Among the many boxes of clothing sent by our Springfield and Boston friends was one from Mr. Wilcox, the Springfield milliner, filled with Shaker bonnets. The little negroes did not know how to put them on, but they liked them so well that they would not take them off, and the school presented a queer appearance to our guests, who could not know our reason for permitting this breach of decorum.

The white people of Edisto have indeed suffered, but now their homes are to be given back to them. The island negroes and those brought here by our bewildered, blundering Government have had, and will have, harder days than their masters. Among those that we have known, however painful their experience, and whether accustomed formerly to easy routine as house-servants or to rougher field service, not one among them would choose ease with servitude rather than suffering with freedom.

In October we saw at the wharf several sickly looking families sitting round fires, waiting for the steamer to carry them off. Two persons who had died in the night from fever and exposure were lying on the bare ground. In the building which we were to use for our school, were two families in a terrible condition. One mother, who was dying, had seven half-naked and half-starved children. All these people had been too sick to leave by the last boat and had crawled back here. Mr. Alden had them taken care of and fed, for they had already used their small crop for food. Mr. Hubbard, of Boston, to whom I wrote, sent me a bale of blankets to distribute among them.

Added to their natural dislike to serve their old masters, many of them have had bitter experiences, which increase their unwillingness. One, named

Venus, told us that she had just come from the "Main," where she had been working all summer; she said: "I put my finger to pencil to sign contract to work all summer for one tenth of the crop, and when it was harvested, I had one quart of molasses and one bushel of corn, and I and my family were sent away." She added that she never would work for a "Secesh" again. Many of them were industrious. One warm day in December when we were looking for a pupil on the Townsend place, who, we were told, lived in "The last nigger house on Nigger Street," we went into a cabin, where a woman was so busy at a cotton-gin that she did not turn her head when she greeted us. We asked how much cotton she could gin a day. "Don' no, missis, no 'casion for to task myself now; Rebs gone."

Occasionally they were glad to see their old masters, but I sometimes saw the "How dy" and outstretched hand rejected. Meeting after meeting was held to reconcile them to the changed and difficult conditions. On one occasion, when explanations only seemed to create greater antagonism, I ventured a remark, and was quickly told by Ishmael, their leader, that I had "Better go into the house and attend to study," thus showing early in his life as freedman, that he had learned the proper sphere of woman.

In February, when we went to the Middleton place to pack the trunks which belonged to Miss Kempton and Miss Stanton, we saw all the negroes coming in from the fields, their hoes over their shoulders. They told us that the guard had ordered them to leave the plantation if they would not agree to work for the owners. Sorely troubled they appealed to us. We could only tell them to obey orders. After this many of the Sherman negroes left the island.

In the spring I went home for a month to see my father, leaving my sister to help Emily with the school.

During the winter and spring, planters were coming and going to arrange with the government representative for their repossession. Many of them were gentlemen, who came into our school and whom we entertained at our table, but when they were in possession and were joined by their families, it was different. The women ignored us.

In May we moved to the bay with our school benches and books, and had a large school there, but a month later the Freedmen's Bureau was dissolved and we were notified that our services were no longer needed. As we were so well established, we obtained permission from the Superintendent of Schools in Charleston to continue, although our large salary of twenty dollars a month was stopped. My salary had always been paid through the Bureau by Mr. Charles Hubbard, of Boston, whose pleasure it was to be responsible for one teacher.

Mr. Alden was dismissed and the island was again under military supervision.

We closed the school in July, but the heat was so intense that we did not wish to travel until it was cooler.

In September we returned the "Union" horse and confiscated carry-all, which had served us and the smallpox patients, and sent to Governor Aiken his furniture which we had bought from the negroes; one piece was the armchair given him by his mother when he was elected governor of South Carolina.

The houses all about us were occupied by Edisto families, who had taken possession of their own. Mr. Edings, the owner of the house we had lived in both summers, wrote that he too wanted to come back. There was no place for us, and in the last week of September, 1866, we said good-by to Edisto and our negro friends.